CLARITY IS POWER

Q & A

"Clarity is Power" book series, is a collection of wisdom from thought-provoking Q and A with renowned Mahatria. His unique gift of answering questions spontaneously is captured in this book, offering life-changing insights.

The "Clarity is Power" series comprises 11 illuminating volumes, each addressing essential aspects of life:

1. Attitudes
2. Self-Discipline
3. Emotional Development
4. Relationships
5. Marriage
6. Parenting
7. Student Life
8. Career Growth
9. Leadership and Entrepreneurship
10. Spirituality
11. Faith

Mahatria Spiritualist | Thought leader | Diviner of infinitheism

For nearly three decades, Mahatria has empowered millions worldwide to achieve holistic abundance. His profound wisdom uplifts people in health, wealth, love, bliss, and spirituality.

infinitheism, the path divined by Mahatria, inspires breakthroughs for anyone who ardently desires abundance by transforming the human spirit to have faith in its infinite potential.

First published in India

MANJUL

Manjul Publishing House

• 2nd Floor, Usha Preet Complex,
42 Malviya Nagar, Bhopal 462 003 - India
• C-16, Sector 3, Noida, Uttar Pradesh 201301 – India
Website: www.manjulindia.com

Distribution Centres:
Ahmedabad, Bengaluru, Bhopal, Kolkata, Chennai,
Hyderabad, Mumbai, New Delhi, Pune

In association with:

infinitheism

3, 3rd Cross Road, R A Puram,
Chennai, Tamil Nadu, India
www.infinitheism.com

EMOTIONAL DEVELOPMENT (CLARITY IS POWER)

by

mahātria Rā

This edition first published in 2016
Third impression 2024

ISBN 978-93-5543-436-4

Printed and bound in India by Thomson Press (India) Ltd.

CLARITY IS POWER

Q & A

EMOTIONAL DEVELOPMENT

mahātria

CONTENTS

CONTENTS

1

> *With so many problems in life, how does one overcome worries and tensions?*

Worries are of two kinds:

1. Those over which we have control.

2. Those over which we have no control.

There's no point in worrying about issues that we have no control over; after all, we cannot do anything about them. And there's no point in worrying about issues over which we have control; after all, we can do something about them. Either way, there is no point in worrying. At birth, we didn't know how to worry. Worrying is a habit that we learnt. Anything that can be learnt can be unlearnt; anything that is acquired can also be dropped. First, understand the futility of worrying and then, just drop it.

'So many problems in life...' is a very bold statement. What problems are you talking about? Did you face earthquakes, cyclonic storms, floods, riots, terminal illness, accidents that left you paralysed, etc... what sort of problems?

Human ego thrives on the fairy tales it can create about the problems of life. Despite what our ego deceives us into believing, the majority of our problems are optional. Most of what we call problems, small or big, are self-created. You are creating a problem when you notice the little red light on your dashboard blinking, but choose to postpone taking the car for an oil change. You may act upset when the car stops midway in rush-hour traffic, but it won't change the fact that you now have a self-created problem. While spending beyond our means, while overusing our credit cards, we are creating a future problem for ourselves. We are aware that when we constantly postpone the nurturing of the most important relationships in our life, problems of resentment or even estrangement will eventually arise. We allow little challenges and inconveniences to grow into upsetting and unnecessary problems everyday. Why should the computer show the same error message every time you boot the system, even three months later?

Of course, problems like natural calamities or the tragedy of terminal illness may be beyond an individual's control. But most of the other issues are self-created. The forest fire we face today is the little spark we overlooked yesterday. Most of today's problems are yesterday's challenges overlooked.

You must first overcome these trivial, day-to-day nuisances. Day-to-day trivialities rob you of your energy. With a little consistency in your lifestyle, some discipline and systematic living, most of these routine trifles can be overcome. Human predicament is that we overestimate our problems and underestimate our ability to trounce them.

Also, you need to change your attitude towards the challenges of life. Life's challenges aren't there to stifle you. In fact, they serve you and help you discover who you are. Challenges actually oblige you, for, when conquered, they help you chase greater challenges and in turn provide you greater growth.

If the British hadn't ruled India, life would've never provided the context for the barrister to discover the Mahatma Gandhi within him. But for the impoverished and those dying on the streets, the school teacher wouldn't have discovered the Mother Teresa within her. All great men were ordinary men who were forced by circumstances to meet great challenges. History is full of simple human beings who won over forces well beyond their control and emerged as champions.

Get your perspective towards worries, tensions and problems right, and you will get your life right. Stop worrying and start living. ●

2

How can I keep myself stable even when the situation does not warrant that?

I remember an incident that happened long time back and I will build the answer on that. A property was negotiated to be purchased and somehow the potential seller was not behaving properly with a potential buyer. So, the potential buyer was getting very angry with the potential seller. I remember asking the potential buyer, 'After you buy this property, are you going to continue to have a relationship with those who sold it to you?' The buyer replied, "There is no relationship with them before this and after this transaction. I don't think I will see them again." Immediately I told him, "Don't waste your anger on somebody with whom you are not going to relate in the future."

We give away our emotions, our tears so easily to people in situations. There must be a premium on your tears. If somebody is ever going to give you a sleepless night, he/she must be worth it in life. We get depressed because somebody passed a comment; we get disturbed because somebody opinionated. Anybody can create nervousness in us, anybody can shake us up, anything can make us cry, and we give away our happiness for silly reasons. Your happiness is the divine part of you; do not give it away to the world for a relationship that's not even worth it. Your tears should not be wasted on that one person who was nasty to you. Do not give it to those who have betrayed you.

Of all the creations of God, a human being alone has been bestowed with this ability to shed those emotional tears. Let your tears roll down in extreme devotion; God is worth your tears... Get so touched by the power of human spirit and let its triumph shed tears. Out of love when you receive a loving expression, shed tears. Whenever I experience a soul that is so pure and I know this world is progressing towards a future on the strength of these few beings who are so pure, I give my tears to them. They are positive tears.

Out of the billions of life forms created by God, he created you as a unique creation called human being and bestowed certain faculties within you and one of those is shedding tears; so there should be a premium to those tears. Will you take 5,000 rupees and just dump it somewhere? I bet, you won't. How come you seem to understand the value of money but not the value of your emotions, your tears? So, develop this enormous strength not to get shaken up in any circumstances or situations by bringing this resolve into yourself - 'I am not going to give away my emotions that easily to anything or anybody.' ●

At birth, we didn't know how to worry. Worrying is a habit that we learnt. Anything that can be learnt can be unlearnt; anything that is acquired can also be dropped.

mahātria

3

If I am called to speak in a function I will happily run towards the dais, but my brother hates such situations. Why do each of us respond differently for the same situation? Why is every human being so different from each other?

If we can understand the circuit of human physiology, then we will understand what causes human behaviour, we will understand, why every human being is so different from the other.

Let us understand the circuit of human physiology:

1. We collect stimuli from the world outside through the five sense organs. Form through the eyes, sound through the ears, taste through the tongue, smell through the nose and touch through the skin. This stimulus is given to the mind/intellect combination within us for processing.

2. The mind/intellect combination examines into memory to find out what has been my response to such a stimuli in the past. In conjunction to my past responses, my mind/intellect, instigates a response to the world outside through my five organs of action namely, vocal cord (speech), legs, hands, genital organs (reproduction and sensuality) and anus (excretion).

3. This very response is again stored in my memory serving future references. Every experience stored in my memory is a combination of,

a) The stimuli,

b) The response and

c) The feeling during the experience/to the experience.

Let us take an example and analyse the above three points that we just discussed.

You see a book in front of you. The eyes having picked up this stimulus gives it to the mind/intellect combination for processing. The mind/intellect combination refers into the memory to find out what has been the response to such a stimuli in the past. The response in the past being picking up the book with your hands and reading it, a similar response is instigated now too. So your hands (one of the organs of action) picks up the book and you start reading. While reading is your response, the feeling you get in reading may either be enjoyable or frustrating (though personally I know it will be the former).

Now this experience of reading and the associated feeling (enjoyable or frustrating) gets stored in your memory for future references.

Let us assume that this reading experience of this book was an enjoyable experience to you and a frustrating experience to your brother. The next time the very sight of the book would instigate you to pick up again and read, for your past experience has been enjoyable. On the contrary your brother would shun the very sight of that book for it was frustrating to him. This explains the differences in human behaviour, the differences prompted by the feelings associated to the experiences.

So, while the stimuli from the world outside remain the same, the difference in response from one person to and other person varies due to the differences in the perception and feelings stored in the memory. This is what the field of psychology calls conditioning.

Every cell in the memory constitutes of the stimuli, the triggered response and the feeling during the experience. If the feeling during the experience was positive you desire to repeat and re-experience those experiences. If the feeling during the experience was negative, you want to avoid responses to those stimuli and you want to avoid the repetition of such experiences. The accumulation of similar experiences and the associated feelings to these experiences are called conditioning.

If, in the past when you spoke in public, your audience applauded your performance and you felt euphoric at their applause and a few similar experiences to the same effect, you get conditioned to look forward to public speaking. You want to grab every possible opportunity to go up the dais. Same is the case with every single thing that you look forward to do in your life. You desire more and more of that which generates pleasurable feelings in you.

It may be the contrary in your brother's case. In his first experience of speaking in public he might have been mocked at by the audience and the feeling could have been one of embarrassment. From then on he would begin to avoid the very thought of speaking in the public. A few similar negative experiences in facing the audience and then he would be conditioned to fear public speaking. Same is true with every single thing that you want to avoid in life. You fear and resist that which generates painful feelings in you.

Conditioning born out of accumulated pleasure creates in you the desire for gain and conditioning born out of accumulated pain creates in you fear of loss. In essence, pleasure and pain are the navigators of human behaviour.

So, if one has to change oneself or change the people around you, working on changing the stimuli from the world outside or changing the response to the world outside is not going to create any lasting change at all. The only way to change is to change the conditioning within a person, out of which the response to the world outside changes.

A short-tempered person, trying to change his angry response to the world or trying to avoid people and circumstances that stimulates anger in him, still find no lasting change within him. Instead, he becomes only more angry about his inability to give up anger. The only solution to conquer anger is to change the conditioning within the person that causes anger. Whether it is emotions like anger, hatred, jealousy, envy that you want to drop or qualities like composure, appreciation, empathy that you want to add or it is habits like smoking, drinking, chewing, procrastination that you want to overcome or you want to transform yourself into organised, healthy, peaceful, blissful, successful... the only way to create a permanent transformation in oneself is to bring about a change in the conditioning of the person.

4

I notice people of varied age groups and stature creating attention-seeking drama. Why do people need so much attention?

Attention-seeking isn't something to complain about. This is but, human frailty. This is something that needs compassion and understanding. After all, we too go through this predicament.

One of the deepest of human cravings is the need to be heard and the need to be attended to. Why? In our growing years, we were obviously not self-sufficient in terms of our self-image and self-esteem. We were dependent on our world. The more attention we received, the more we felt wanted. In most cases, even after we have grown into adults, we are still not self-sufficient when it comes to our self-image and self-esteem. In that sense, we are just a child in an adult body. Consequently, most of us have a tendency to perform attention-seeking drama.

This is one place where dogs score over humans. Whenever you return, your dog greets you by jumping on you, wagging its tail, licking you. It gives you so much attention and makes you feel very important. No wonder we call it our pet. Pet animals, we have in abundance. Pet humans, is what we lack.

Haven't you noticed the new breed of swimmers creating big splashes, with their strokes, to gain attention?

Haven't you seen people shifting to sleeveless T-shirts at the slightest appearance of biceps? What about the man who doesn't wear the top buttons of his shirt so as to display his hairy chest? A new mobile user makes it so obvious by allowing it to ring long enough before taking the call, and by speaking in a tone loud enough for others to hear, so as to draw attention.

Some come up with top notch performances to be the cause for celebration, while others resort to pranks to be celebrated; some laugh to get noticed, while others cry to draw attention. 'Show off' is the common man's name for such people. They are basically attention seekers. In fact, in some ways, all of us are attention seekers.

Owing to this inadequacy in self-esteem and self-image, we need the attention of the world in order to feel complete; by ourselves, we are incomplete. It's not enough that we know what we've done is good. We need the world to endorse what we've done. Our own success gives us a sense of accomplishment only when others applaud it. Awards and rewards give us a sense of fulfilment because they confirm that we've drawn enough attention.

A world-renowned spiritual teacher once remarked, "Let the media write good things about me or bad things about me... I don't care. But they must keep writing about me. I must be in the news." In America, a man randomly shot at people on the street, wounding many and killing a few. He later said, "I didn't know how else to make the headlines in the newspaper." When we don't know the right way to gain attention, we resort to any available way to gain it. Seeking fame is nothing more than man's desperation to be the centre of all attention. Why else will I walk in public wearing clothes that aren't even adequate for the bedroom? Attention seekers can be found everywhere, and many of us are no exception.

The point is that there is a tender heart within each of us that needs attention. If the child within us is not given attention, we resort to childish behaviour (even as adults) to draw that attention. A hungry man needs food, not criticism. Seeking attention is a sort of psychological hunger... and very few are exempt from it.

When old people at home are constantly complaining about their ailments, it is not just physical... it is psychosomatic. There is a psychological craving for attention. That's why, offering to take our loved ones to the doctor, instead of asking them to go by themselves, makes all the difference. The very offer of accompanying them to see the doctor, rather than sending them with the driver, has a healing touch. It has been observed that the healing is faster when you give the medicine to your loved ones, rather than letting them take it by themselves. People need that touch of love, and they experience it only when they feel they are being attended to.

The teenager at home is not bad, but is exhibiting bad behaviour because he is not getting enough attention. We take a well-behaved child for granted, don't we? It's not that your daughter cannot study by herself; it's just that she enjoys the attention she gets when you sit along with her to study. It's not that the adolescent at home wants to speak on the phone for 45 minutes; what we need to understand here is that for those 45 minutes, someone at the other end of the phone is making your daughter feel like a princess. Children drift away from parental control when someone in the world makes them feel more wanted than their parents. When children get enough attention, when they get enough appreciation for all their positives, when every little improvement of theirs is encouraged, when there is enough quality time and communication between parents and children... there will hardly be any emotional tantrum.

The solution is simple: To all the people who matter to you and to whom you matter, take the initiative to give them enough attention, preferably, to their positive qualities. Be demonstrative. Be vocal. Develop expressiveness. Invest quality time. Shower them with lavish praise. Give them a lot of encouragement. Make your presence in the relationship adequately felt.

The next time you hear a complaint, be compassionate. Somebody needs your attention. The next time you witness an emotional drama, be compassionate. Somebody needs your attention. ●

5

How to deal with immature people?

There are a lot of limitations in people. You can either be affected by it or you can actually feel compassionate towards them. The former will leave you disturbed, and the latter will make you peaceful. The choice is yours and yours only.

For example, some people are disrespectful not because they disrespect you; it is ego fulfilling for them to be so. They somehow feel by putting you down, their ego gets satiated. It's their inadequacy but you're taking it so personal and letting it affect you.

Understand that every immature behaviour you see in others is their inadequacy and not yours. If you are suffering because of your weakness something can be done. But getting affected by others' immaturity and weakness is insanity.

Some people will criticize, irrespective of whatever you do. To criticize is their weakness, their inadequacy. Unless they criticize others, they are not comfortable with themselves. It's strange how, some people achieve ego fulfillment through criticism.

While 99% of us will come into Instagram and Facebook or YouTube for our growth, there are some people who will come only to create nuisance through their bad criticism, comments, and abusive language. They achieve nothing by doing so except for some momentary attention, leaving behind a bad aftertaste. Their ego fulfillment comes only by disturbing other people. It is their weakness and inadequacy, and it has nothing to do with you.

Getting affected by fools turns you into another fool and we need to recognize this. You can only feel compassionate towards these people. Understand that they have chosen a path of ego fulfillment, which is never going to develop them.

In all those moments when I come across immature behaviour, I tell myself this and feel liberated – *"Uska maturity uthna hi hai!"* ("Their maturity is just that much!"). It is such a magical liberating mindset to live your life with.

When you're stuck in a traffic jam with 25 cars in front of you and the signal is red and somewhere from behind you somebody honks - *"Keeeeek"*. There is only one way of responding – *"Uska maturity uthna hi hai!"* and feel compassionate towards them.

The world relates to you according to their maturity levels. You relate to the world according to your maturity levels.

Consider yourself mature, if and only if, the immaturity of others does not disturb you.

There is so much happiness and liberation in recognising: *'Uska maturity uthna hi hai!'* (Their maturity is just that much!). •

During the final year of my college, I was involved in a relationship only to be betrayed by the man later. I am now caught up in this guilt and confusion - should I reveal everything about my past to the person I will eventually marry?

Two monks were walking when they spotted a teenage girl standing by the stream they were about to cross. The young girl had fear written all over her face. It was already dusk, and daylight was fading. In response to the question one of the monks had asked, the girl replied, "I am afraid of crossing the stream." The monk volunteered to carry the girl on his shoulders. He dropped her on the other side and the two monks continued to walk.

After they had walked for about 30 minutes, noting a sense of unease in the other monk, the monk who had helped the young girl asked him if something was bothering him. The other monk retorted, "Don't you know that monks aren't supposed to touch the opposite sex? Why then did you carry the girl on your shoulders? That's why I am upset." Centred and still smiling, the monk who had helped the girl replied, "Oh, the girl you are talking about... I dropped her a long time back. Why are you still carrying her in your head?"

Your past has left you a long time back; yet you continue to carry it in your head and continue to be affected by it. You can help a person caught in the jaws of a crocodile. But how can you help a person who thinks she is caught in the jaws of a crocodile, while all she has is just the picture of a crocodile under her feet? The past has no reality, except in the memory in which it is processed. Carrying is an effort. Dropping is a decision. Make a decision and drop it. Life should be a forward progression, and not a backward regression. Save your future from the clutches of your past.

To unburden yourself of your past, first and foremost, embrace forgiveness. Gautama Buddha and Jesus Christ had the same views on this aspect. "Hatred does not cease by hatred; hatred ceases only by love," claimed one, and the other said, "Love your enemies." The one who has hurt you in life has gone on with his/her life, but you continue to drown yourself in the memories of what has happened, ruining your todays, your peace of mind, your sleep, your happiness and above all, your precious health. Remember, between the hated and the hater, it is always the hater who suffers more. One of the most selfish things you can do in life is to forgive the other and thus liberate yourself from the clutches of hatred... after all, it is the hater who suffers more.

Guilt is as much a retardant as hurt. Liberate yourself from both. When you don't forgive the other, you suffer from hurt; when you can't forgive yourself, you suffer from guilt. Remind yourself that you are only human, and humans err... With a resolve not to repeat the same mistake, forgive yourself too for the mistakes of your past... which might have hurt others. 'To forgive is divine' also means 'self-forgiveness'.

Forgive others and forgive yourself too. Unless you forgive, you cannot forget... Give pardon and get peace of mind. A little pain in one part of the body should not stop the functioning of the entire body. Something that had gone wrong during a certain phase of your life shouldn't halt the progress of your life.

Yesterday was over yesterday, and that's the reality. Draw a line over your past and move on. Today is a new day. When bad things happen to good people, they become better people. This is the plan on which life is built. A saying goes - 'Today can be the last day of your life'. True. Equally true is the fact that today is the first day of the rest of your life. The beginning is from where you begin. Begin today. Begin now. Begin here and move on. The person you will become in life is already waiting for you in the future. Go and meet him/her.

Should I reveal everything about my past to the man I will eventually marry? True, I have reiterated it many times - 'Intimacy in relationship can be built only by being transparent in a relationship'. However, I also want to clarify that most people are not mature enough to deal with transparency. You need a certain level of maturity to accept the transparency of people and not hold it against those who have been honest with you. Dealing with honesty needs a level of maturity, and I don't think we still live in such a mature world (I am not sure we will ever!) That's why we need churches for confessions and the husband or wife isn't enough!

The very fact that you have drawn a line over your past, means your past is no more. It's a dream over... okay, a nightmare over. Why speak of a dream to someone whom we do not know for sure can handle it? After all, none of us will know everything about each other even with the best of intentions to be transparent. Our own memories will fail us. There is no sinner without a future and no saint without a past. Leave what is over as over. Don't give it a renewed life.

What about intimacy then? Practice transparency in the present continuous. Let us talk about today, today and not about yesterday, today. In fact, it is a mantra for peaceful life and great relationships - talk about today, today and not about yesterday, today. ●

“

***Guilt is as much a retardant as hurt.
Liberate yourself from both.
Forgive others and
forgive yourself too.***

mahātria

7

Why can't we live just on the basis of our instincts, why do we have to suppress everything, for example our anger?

Suppressing anger is not a solution. In fact, it takes greater amount of energy to hold your emotions than to express it. Emotions born but not expressed do not get buried dead, but get buried alive. All suppressed emotions keep burning from within. Continuous suppression of anger, or for that matter any emotion, accumulates into emotional baggage and they come out in ugly and unmanageable proportions in the most unexpected circumstances. So, suppressing anger is not the solution but transcending anger is.

First understand anger. Anger is not a result of what the world does to you. Anger is the basic expression of your inability to be in control of the situation in any other way. Whenever the current situation is not in your control you let your temper loose.

In the animal kingdom, the only way to keep oneself away from being hurt by the rest is by exhibiting anger. "Come no further; this hurts; this is my space; I do not want to be disturbed," and many more of these expressions can only be communicated to others through anger. Anger is their defence mechanism. Anger in human beings is that animal expressing itself. When through human ways we are not able to take control of a situation, we resort to the animal in us.

So the primary understanding is that anger is not born out of any deficiency with others, but out of your own inadequacy to be in control of a situation. It is not that he is not doing what I want him to do. It is that I am not able to get him to do what I want. So I become angry. Anger is more a message to you than to the world. Anger tells you to look into some inadequacy that is there in you. So, how do I transcend anger?

Awareness! It is through awareness and awareness alone that you can transcend anger. Every time you get angry, become aware of it. Ask yourself the following questions: Whom are you primarily destroying with your anger; isn't it yourself? What did you get in return? A small job was done, and acids got secreted in your body; is it worth it? What was your personal inadequacy that led to this anger? Was there another way, a better way, a humane way in which you could have handled the situation? If need be, maintain a pocket journal with you in which you can record your awareness and realisations during every bout of your anger.

The more and more you find answers to the above questions, the lesser will be the intensity of your anger. Over a period of time, you would have not only conquered your anger but would have also evolved into a much better person, equipped in enough human ways to take control of any situation. ●

Anger is not a result of
what the world does to you.
Anger is the basic expression
of your inability
to be in control of the situation
in any other way.

mahātria

8

How to assess whether I am on the right track?

You can never comprehend whether you are on the right track or not, by comparing yourself with other people. You can never be the other. You can only be yourself. You do not benchmark yourself with others, but you do benchmark yourself with your value system.

There are those whose values are life-based. With every new situation, they will change their values. In reality, what can change with circumstances cannot be called values. Value-based living is the right way and not life-based values.

There is a 'Knower' in each of us. That's the value-based self. There is a 'Doer' in each of us. That's the self that acts in the world. As long as there is no split between the 'Knower' and 'Doer' within you, you are on the right track. If there is a split then you are on the wrong track. ●

9

At times, I feel little disappointed about people's ingratitude. Is it wrong to expect gratitude?

I do not want to assume people are ungrateful. I wish to believe that most people live with gratitude, even though they may not be saying it. Just that the tongue is not spelling out all that the heart feels. The tongue cannot spell out all the feelings. True feelings are beyond words. The lower can attempt, but can never truly express the higher.

The moment you offer a chocolate to a child, his excitement to eat it is far greater than to tell you 'Thank You'. But isn't watching the child eating the chocolate with so much excitement a reward in itself? Wasn't that the very purpose for which you got the chocolate or was it to listen to a 'Thank you'?

You gave a breakthrough to her and she has gone on to scale great heights in her career. What greater reward for your initiative than this? Why do the good, and then expect something in reciprocation and end up being disappointed? What's the point? The purpose for which you gave, when that is fulfilled, that's a far greater reward than any verbal articulation.

People are not ungrateful. We are basically not a very expressive generation. Our primary relationship is with technology. Even our relationship with people has become primarily through technology. As a result, the prime casualty has been our expressions. There is no smile in a smiley. LOL doesn't reverberate. SMS hugs and e-hugs lack the warmth of touch. Human to human, emotions have a different depth; through technology it can only be shallow.

The primary issue is not ingratitude but lack of expressiveness and demonstrativeness. As a generation we are losing out on the ability to make our feelings visible. That's why we struggle even to write personal letters, and we rely on the greeting card industry to express ourselves. That's why we need Mother's Day, Valentine's Day, Thanksgiving Day etc., a day to trigger the expression of appropriate emotions. We being so expressive on such days is a consolation that feelings have not been lost; just the expressions have been lost.

By expecting anything from others, the fulfilment of which is not in your control, you are inviting disappointments. So do not expect gratitude. However, what you expect from the world, when you expect it from yourself, you can control it and hence fulfil it. So, always express your gratitude to the world. Simply put, forget what you have done for the world. Never expect gratitude. Never forget what the world has done for you. Never fail to express gratitude.

“

By expecting anything from others,
the fulfilment of which
is not in your control,
you are inviting disappointments.
So do not expect gratitude.

mahātria

So often people don't seem
what they appear. We believe
a person to be something,
but they turn out to be
something else altogether.
In such a world,
how do we learn to trust?

Irrespective of what happened to you yesterday, irrespective of what you did to the world or what the world did to you, you have to wake up every morning and trust this world all over again. I know it is easier said than done, but you don't have a choice because your peace is entwined in your trust. Without trust there is no peace. Distrust leaves you distressed.

In the thousands of times you may travel by public transport your wallet may be picked from your pocket once or twice. Even when you don't trust the world and check your wallet every few minutes, still some competent thief would anyway get the better of you and pick your pocket some day; but, it would have cost you a thousand opportunities to be otherwise peaceful. The eyes that see every co-passenger as a potential thief, would have ruined your peace thousands of times, while trusting the world would have made every journey peaceful. Be wise and not otherwise.

A Nathuram Godse will get his way through, but in seeing everyone as a potential Godse you will miss a million Gandhians. Not worth it. In search of one Osama you will have to doubt every noble heart. Not worth it. Let us have security systems in place, let us have foolproof systems, let us raise above our vulnerabilities, let us lock the cars and tie the horses, but above all in the interest of our own peace, let us trust the world all over again.

One employee will betray your trust. Still trust the rest. One customer will default. Still trust the rest. One supplier will cheat. Still trust the rest. A key relationship will take your goodness to be your weakness, and your trust may be exploited. Wake up another morning and start trusting all over again. I may be sounding naive, but I am showing you the gates of peace, which opens only with the keys of trust.

It is not about whether the world is good or not, whether the world is trustworthy or not, but it is about whether you want to be peaceful or not. There is only one way to peace - T.R.U.S.T.

Whenever I have been cheated or betrayed or exploited or hurt, I have always told myself, "Thank god that I was cheated, but I wasn't the cheat; I was betrayed, but I didn't betray; I was hurt, but I didn't hurt. Let me suffer the wrong, but never inflict the wrong."

Let us assume every morning that the world will be trustworthy from today. Even if the world betrays our trust, let us wake up to another day and trust this world all over again. A zillion times the world will live up to our trust and a few hundred times it will let us down. The odds are tremendously in our favour.

"

It is not about whether the world is good or not, whether the world is trustworthy or not, but it is about whether you want to be peaceful or not.

mahātria

11

My father was a very healthy person but he developed some health complications and in less than a month we lost him. I am not able to reconcile with this loss. How to come out of it?

I do empathise with your tears. I know how it feels when you lose a loved one. But tell me, my dear, can any of us escape death? We all have come with confirmed return tickets, just that we do not know the date on it.

There are a few legitimate sufferings in life, which time alone can heal. Time will progressively de-intensify the pain of losing... memories will remain, but the feelings will subside. Feelings have a short lifespan. Unlike memories, time will fade the feelings away. You have to go through this phase of legitimate pain of having lost your beloved father... there is no escaping it. But time will heal you.

How you feel is one thing, but feel good for your father. He embraced a peaceful death. Die... all of us must, but embracing a peaceful death is such a great blessing. Die... all of us will, sooner or later, but will it be a suffering end or a peaceful end? Your father, now or later, had to go... but isn't it good for him that it was so peaceful and he didn't have to endure suffering and then eventually die. Feel good for your father.

In the meanwhile, I want you to be aware that life is actually benevolent. It gives you, allows you to enjoy it and only then it takes it back. Life gave you a father, allowed you to enjoy your father for several years and only then took back your father. Though it has taken back your father, it has not taken away the memories you carry about your father. Till now you enjoyed him in the physical reality. Continue to enjoy him in the mental reality. Cherish the memories of him. Play and replay this mental game with your father endlessly.

Even God cannot stop you from living with your father in your own mental world. At the end of everyday, have some quite moments with your father. Just stay connected to him. Open your eyes and you live in one world. Close your eyes and you live in another world. And in that world, your memories are the monarch. Till you live, your father will live in your mental world. Right now close your eyes, and see, he is always with you... always will be with you... and that, even God cannot take him away from you.

Leo Buscaglia, a soul that lived propagating love, returned from his father's funeral, and he found at his doorstep a bouquet of flowers, a bar of chocolate and an anonymous note. "This is just to remind you, even after your father's death, there are still beautiful things to see and sweet things to eat. Your life is still on... live on... With love."

I say the same unto you. Your life is still on... live on... and live on, so that your father's soul delights in seeing the way you live... ●

“

Feelings have a short lifespan.
Unlike memories,
time will fade the feelings away.

mahātria

12

If I do not approve of the other's opinion in a discussion it shows up immediately on my face. How to avoid that? Is diplomacy a virtue?

You are basically saying how to stop being truthful. When you don't like it let the world know that you don't like it. Why should you be diplomatic? If diplomacy means being untruthful to your emotions, then it is not a virtue. Thinking something and expressing something else is not diplomacy; it is hypocrisy. You don't have to project yourself as somebody whom you are not.

Dale Carnegie said, '90% of the people live 90% of their lives projecting to the world that they are not'. I agree with him totally. 'I should look right in the eyes of the world' seems to more dominant in you, rather than 'I should think right and feel right'. You want to appear good in others' opinion. I want you to 'be' good. Let the striving be that. Over time people will see goodness in you.

Be spontaneous in your expressions. Strive to be good by having the right thoughts and feelings. When you are thinking and feeling right and when you are spontaneous, can those expressions of spontaneity be wrong? Projecting a falsehood will rob you of peace; being truthful to your emotions will make you lot more peaceful. The striving should be to clean up the inside of the bottle, so that it looks clean from outside too. Then no projections will be needed.

In projecting a falsehood to the world, you are actually creating a split within yourself. That split will hurt you internally. True freedom is to express what you think; to experience this freedom, groom yourself to have right thoughts and feelings. When the intentions and the motive is right, then the spontaneous expressions will also be right.

In being truthful and not hiding your emotions, sometimes the world will misunderstand you. But if it is born out of right intentions, then eventually the world will understand. In fact people will trust you and relate more with you for your honesty.

Be honest. Strive to have right thoughts and feelings. Be expressive. Gift yourself peace in the process. ●

*True freedom is to express
what you think;
to experience this freedom,
groom yourself
to have right thoughts and feelings.
When the intentions
and the motive is right,
then the spontaneous expressions
will also be right.*

mahātria

Ego is a motivator!
How can ego bring
down a person?

Whether ego brings down a person or not, it certainly brings down the peace of a person. The flipside of ego is that it craves for attention. Ego, for its survival, thrives on attention. The craving is to get noticed. Everyone goes through this phase, where the ego drives one to do anything and everything only to get noticed and recognised. It is a phase when good is good only when it gains attention; even bad is good if it can draw attention, and ironically, even good is bad if it fails to attract attention. The ego survives on gaining attention. But then, one must outgrow that phase of life; if not, the price you pay will be your peace.

True, ego can be a source of motivation; but then, ego is a very poor motivator. By its very nature, ego needs feeding; and hence it makes you a perpetual beggar. The problem with ego is that when ego is fed, you struggle out of superiority complex, and when ego is starved you suffer out of inferiority complex. Either way, it robs you of your peace of mind. The price ego asks of you to be your motivator is your peace of mind. Why would you sell your hair to buy a comb?

Every moment is heavy, every situation is nerve-racking, every interaction is tense... an ego-filled heart is always walking on fire. Never can there be a moment of marriage between ego and ease. Ego is never worth the losses. With ego, you are struggling all the time to win over the situation; you want to get the better of others. When you transcend ego, you just want to win over yourself; you want to make the most of your own potential. There is enormous freedom in letting your ego go.

A crow carrying a piece of meat in its beak found itself being chased by all the other birds. It dropped the piece of meat, and all the birds went after the meat. Now, alone in the sky, the crow remarked, "In losing that piece of meat, I gained the freedom of the skies." The piece of meat is ego. And, the freedom is your peace.

When ego comes, everything else goes. When ego goes, everything else comes. ●

“

The ego survives on
gaining attention.
But then, one must outgrow
that phase of life;
if not, the price you pay
will be your peace.

mahātria

14

I cannot remain in a
stress-free, happy state.
I am emotionally
very unstable.
Rude comments and
harsh statements affect me.
Can you help me?

It seems... Near the chocolate counter in the supermarket a little girl was profusely crying. The mother said, "Jennifer, relax. Jennifer, please relax. Don't behave in any way that will leave behind a bad impression." The little daughter's tantrum won't stop. She adds a little scream to her crying. The mother again said, "Jennifer, relax. Don't get overtly perturbed. There is no need for a drama now. Jennifer, just relax." A man, who was observant of what was going on, approached the mother and said, "Madam, I know the little one's behaviour is out of control. Yet, don't you think you are using too much of an adult communication with a six-year-old?" The mother turned towards the man and replied, "What gave you this feeling that I am talking to my little girl? Jennifer is my name. I was actually giving auto-suggestions to myself, to calm me down."

While your success depends on what you communicate with others, your happiness depends on what you communicate to yourself. Whatever be your name, I wish to tell you, "Jennifer, reeelllaaax. Jennifer, just reelllaaaaax." Start this communication with yourself. Multiple times in a day, give auto-suggestion to yourself saying, "Jennifer, relax."

If you want everybody to be happy with you, you will never be at peace with yourself. Being rude and harsh is the limitation of other people. You should not die of other people's cancer. 'Jennifer, relax'. If they don't know to behave, that's their inadequacy. You should not own it up on you. Dogs bark - not at you, but at any moving object. Don't take it too personal. 'Jennifer, relax'.

A piece of wood held too close to the eye would cover the entire sun. Hold it at a distance, and it is just an insignificant piece of wood. Any issue, if taken to the heart, is sure to hurt. Don't give anything in life that exalted status that it can disturb your peace. Put your peace above everything. If you leave petty things as petty, your life will be pretty.

Also understand, it is never 'something' or 'someone' who is making you feel positive or negative, but it is your 'acceptance' or 'non-acceptance' of something or someone, which is making you feel positive or negative. It isn't the world, but the quality of your response to the world (acceptance or non-acceptance) that determines the quality of your emotions. Next time you feel disturbed, instead of asking 'who or what is disturbing me', examine who or what you are resisting (not accepting) that is causing the disturbance in you. Replace resistance (non-acceptance) with acceptance, and the negative emotion will turn into a positive one.